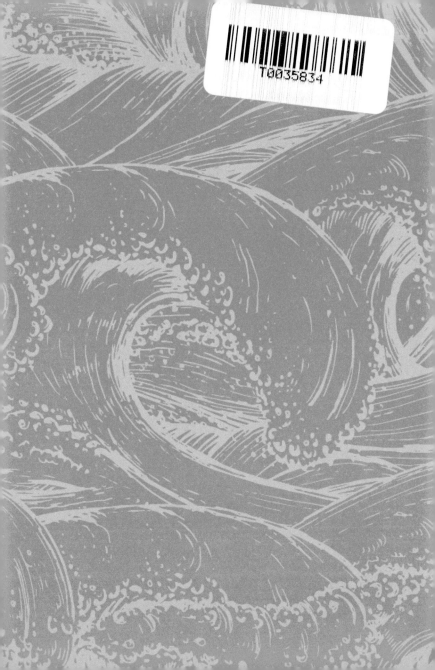

THE
SURFER
AND THE
SAGE

Published by Familius LLC, www.familius.com
PO Box 1249, Reedley, CA 93654

Familius books are available at special discounts for bulk purchases,
whether for sales promotions or for family or corporate use.
For more information, contact Familius Sales at orders@familius.com.

Library of Congress Control Number: 2021950357

Print ISBN 9781641706551
Ebook ISBN 9781641706827

Printed in China

Edited by Peg Sandkam and Sarah Echard
Cover design by Mara Harris
Book design by Mara Harris

10 9 8 7 6 5 4 3 2 1

First Edition

Shaun Tomson & Noah benShea

THE
SURFER
AND THE
SAGE

A Guide to Survive & Ride
Life's Waves

PHOTOGRAPHS BY DAN MERKEL

FAMILIUS

SHAUN TOMSON AT BANZAI PIPELINE, HAWAII

CHAPTERS

Introduction: Waves   1
I: Anxious & Calm   17
II: Despair & Hope   27
III: Doubt & Faith   35
IV: Confusion & Clarity   43
V: Guilt & Forgiveness   51
VI: Isolated & Connected   61
VII: Exhausted & Inspired   69
VIII: Powerless & Empowered   77
IX: Defeated & Unbreakable   89
X: Hubris & Humility   97
XI: Stuck & Liberated   109
XII: Fear & Courage   1119
XIII: Giving Up & Letting Go   131
XIV: Frailty & Resilience   141
XV: Pessimism & Optimism   149
XVI: Tentative & Tenacious   157
XVII: Uncertain & Committed   167
XVIII: Privilege & Gratitude   175
A Final Perspective   183
About the Authors   195
About Familius   196

NORTH SHORE, OAHU, HAWAII

Dedicated to my mother, Marie Tomson (1930–2021).
For love, prayer, and hope—God bless.

—SHAUN TOMSON

For Eli and Samuel
Dor L'Dor

—ZaZa

This world is too often
too broken
for too many.

So we're here to help make
a few repairs.

And help you make
a few of your own.

—SHAUN & NOAH

BACKDOOR PIPELINE, HAWAII

Introduction

WAVES

HONOLUA BAY, MAUI, HAWAII

THE SURFER

Fierce winds whipping across water create waves. For most of the world's six billion people, waves are to be avoided. Waves represent turbulence, danger, power, and powerlessness. Most people in coastal areas want to stay away to remain dry and safe. Surfers, however, live for waves, especially the area where waves focus their energy and break along the shoreline. For good reason, surfers call this area where a wave briefly crests to its highest point and then crashes forward with its maximum energy "the impact zone."

THE SAGE

The next big thing in your life
is already on the way.

You don't have to welcome
its arrival.

Because it is you arriving.

Because it is you heading
toward you.

That's the wave breaking.

Destiny won't just knock
at your door.

It will kick the door down.

And denial can't lock the door.

So here's the action plan.

Hope for the best and make peace
with the rest.

If reality calls, you can't hang up.

Or refuse to answer the phone.

Being on your best behavior simply means being your best you.

Anyone who tells you something else is a snake oil salesman.

And remember how much of an ally the snake was to Adam and Eve.

THE SURFER

There are many waves that travel unseen through our society and our consciousness before rising up and crashing down in the impact zone. A wave of change; a wave of technology; a wave of stress; a wave of opioid abuse; a wave of job losses. A wave is looked at as a vast force, as something out of our control—a macro force that will impact all at a micro level and be responsible for upending nice, stable lives.

I have been a surfer for over fifty years. Along with my contemporaries, I helped create professional surfing and build a surfing industry. Today I work with large organizations, schools, and teams to use the principles of surfing to aid in the practice of leadership. I help connect people to their true purpose and, through a simple process, help individuals engage more effectively with others to ultimately improve individual and group performance.

Surfing and riding waves are at the core of my discussions and workshops. After speaking to hundreds of thousands of people, I understand that the lessons one learns from surfing can help transform attitude, reawaken purpose, activate higher levels of engagement, and, ultimately, improve wellbeing.

I am not a trained psychologist, psychiatrist, coach, social worker, or teacher. My studies are in the field of business and leadership. However, over the years, I have developed a simple system to help individuals activate the power of purpose to make personal change. I often meet individuals who are more interested in survival than finding their purpose and the power to improve their personal performance. They feel they are getting swept along on a wave of malaise, that they are powerlessly trapped in the grip of a powerful wave. For some, just getting through tomorrow is enough . . .

THE SAGE

Time only moves forward.

Tomorrow never arrives.

Never.

Now is the only place
you can find your footing.

And no one ever stood on a
surfboard who didn't fall off.

So when you fall off, get over it.

And get on, and on again.

"Success is a series
of glorious defeats."

—Mahatma Gandhi

And lose the mea culpa.

Too many of us were raised
to think that beating ourselves up
is an act of character.

It's not.

Do not confuse being self-abusive
with being self-accountable.

All self-transformation
requires self-witnessing.

Be an honest witness.

Because you count.

We all count.

And count on each other.

That's just the way life's ocean rolls.

THE SURFER

The ocean has this elemental attraction to us all: Earth is 75 percent water—97 percent of which is seawater—and the blood in our bodies is 60 percent water, with a concentration of salt that is similar to the oceans.

Having ridden more waves than most on this planet, I have always felt that wave-riding skills may help with a philosophy of riding life's waves. I have wondered whether there was a way to write a simple book distilling what I have learned that can help others to find their inner power—to no longer feel powerless—and learn to ride that powerful wave rather than be swept away by it. These thoughts have been percolating in my subconscious, but there was something missing in my knowledge base.

Then, at a meeting over lunch—you know those moments when there is an immediate spiritual connection with another. . .

EDDIE AIKAU AT SUNSET BEACH, HAWAII

THE SAGE

When the Surfer and I met,
it wasn't the first time.

But too many of us too often
confuse meeting for the first time
with meeting at the right time.

When the Surfer and I met,
it was the right time.

And we were like old friends
meeting for the first time.

And it was important.

Why?

Because in this brief life,
on this brief journey,
of all the things you can make in life,
why not make a difference?

And when the Surfer and I met,
it was the right time
to make a difference.

Together.

The last of the human freedoms—
to choose one's own attitude
in any given set of circumstances,
to choose one's own way.

—*VIKTOR FRANKL*

BANZAI PIPELINE, HAWAII

LENNOX HEAD, AUSTRALIA

I

ANXIOUS & CALM

WAIMEA BAY, OAHU, HAWAII

THE SURFER

Anxiety is a jab in the jaw for your attention; it gets your heart beating, your senses tingling, and your body ready for action—it's a jolt of adrenaline straight to the central nervous system.

Right above my childhood bed in my father's apartment overlooking the Bay of Plenty in Durban, South Africa, was a photo of the Banzai Pipeline—the world's most feared wave.

I would get anxious just looking at the picture because I knew that one day I would have to go there to test myself . . .

The waves at the Banzai Pipeline break a short distance from shore, often no more than fifty yards from the coarse sand on which sit thousands of spectators during the winter competition season. Waves are generated by storms hundreds of miles away, and these swells travel through deep water until feeling the resistance of the shallow coral reef at the Pipeline. Waves stack up together into sets, a grouping, each about fifteen seconds apart, and then increase in size as they sweep towards the shore, their force magnified by the shallowing coral reef, changing from swells into waves, whipped ever-higher by the fierce trade winds blowing the spray upwards and out to sea like a rain squall.

As you stand on the beach watching ten- to fifteen-foot waves detonate on the reef, you can feel the concussion through your feet. *Ka-boom—ka-boom.* Surfers paddle for the waves, sometimes blinded by the fierce winds, and launch themselves over the edge of the wave as it rears up vertically on the reef, hoping that their forward momentum, skill, and commitment will keep them on the wave's face and not pitch them forward into the air and a deadly wipeout.

After I would paddle out through the in-rushing waves, sped along by the out-rushing rip current, I would sit and wait for my first ride and consciously suppress the beating of my heart.

Anxiety is caused by a fear of a future occurrence—failure, injury, or even death. Anxiety is a deep dread of failing.

I discovered that anxiety can be controlled, first through breath and then with clearing thoughts. Breathe slowly and deeply, calmly and consciously, and then empty the mind, clear it of all thought. Calmness is like a warming coat for a shivering body, an antidote to fear, a clearing wind to sweep away anxiety.

I would breathe, slowly and deeply, rhythmically, and the fluid motion would still my beating heart, and, through focus and concentration, through thought and control, I would let go of being anxious and find my inner calm. I would bring the fear and anxiety of an uncertain future and potential failure to my locus of control in the present. And then I would start to paddle for the next wave, and my actions and forward motion would dispel the anxiety like a clearing and calming wind . . .

WILD COAST, SOUTH AFRICA

SHAUN TOMSON AT SUNSET BEACH, HAWAII

THE SAGE

The word "anxious" can by itself make you feel anxious. And perhaps no word is more emblematic of how people are feeling these days.

Sadly, anxiety attacks all other feelings no matter if we are talking about love, work, or even aging. Anxiety debilitates our ability to find more and not less in every aspect of our lives. Just as guilt won't change your past, neither will anxiety improve your future.

But what people seldom realize is that anxiety is not necessarily a negative; it's a warning system built into our biopsychology.

Perhaps think of anxiety as a balancing pole that will keep you upright on your "life" board as you witness waves that can threaten to topple you. Anxiety says, "Pay attention." Or else you will pay later.

So how do we find our balance with anxiety? By seeing it for what it is AND isn't. Bottom line: Don't give anxiety too much of your attention because anxiety isn't a boost but a caution. And anxiety won't improve your future.

"Calm," on the other hand, is a word that has been idealized in every religion and teaching across time. Finding that quiet safe place inside of you is about as good as it gets in life. If you doubt this for a moment, imagine a life where your roommate-for-life is anxiety.

Finding calm on your "life" board in the middle of a great ride is a wave's meditation lifting you to a sacred place.

Choose calm when it calms your spirit, but do not choose calm when it robs you of the wild ride that you want to remember for the rest of your life. Make that decision calmly and treasure the moment. But do not confuse calm as being passionless. Or your life will be less.

When there are storms overhead,
drop down into your mind ocean and
ride the waves under your waves.
The calm in your storm
is the calm within you.
Your calm is calmly waiting.
Your calm is not at a distance
from you unless you are at
a distance from you.

—*NOAH BENSHEA*

WAIMEA BAY, OAHU, HAWAII

II

DESPAIR & HOPE

PFEIFFER BEACH, BIG SUR, CALIFORNIA

THE SURFER

A dream is often the ethereal nature of hope come to life in mental images, but for many, when the dream doesn't come true, despair is the result.

My dad's dream of traveling to the 1948 London Olympics and winning a swimming gold medal for his country didn't come true. While waiting for a wave on his wooden surfboard about one hundred yards out from shore at South Beach in Durban, South Africa, a shark came up underneath him and hit him with terrifying force, biting down into his right bicep. He later wrote, "it lifted me clear into the air" and "it was an ideal day for surfing and for sharks."

My father was rushed to the hospital and given blood transfusions and emergency surgery and ultimately survived. He traveled to San Francisco for additional arm surgery and recuperated on Waikiki Beach in Hawaii, where he befriended the Kahanamoku clan, legendary beachboys who had been his swimming heroes.

A founding principle of the beachboy ethos is "Never turn your back on the ocean."

Be aware of the dangers associated with the sea, but never turn your back on its goodness.

I like to think that this simple concept gave my father hope in what could have been a time of deep despair. Hope is a choice, a reframing of the present situation and a positive perspective of the future. Hope is action, the antidote to the inaction of despair.

In one bite, the shark had erased my father's dream. Over the years, I have thought what that might mean to an athlete in his physical prime—poised to be a champion and then no hope of success. What happens when your dream is no longer attainable? Is hope vanquished, and does despair reign?

Is life a spiral downward into despair, a journey forward with a backpack laden with bitterness and hopelessness?

When I think of my father and how he lived his life, I know he constructed a new dream—a dream not of being the best swimmer but rather of helping other people be their best at what they loved.

He helped an entire generation of young surfers realize their potential through emotional and financial support, and I was part of that tribe. My dad reframed his dream into giving hope to others—making their dreams come true.

Three decades after recuperating on the beach at Waikiki, my father traveled back to Hawaii to watch me compete in the Pipeline Masters, the world's most prestigious surfing competition on the world's most dangerous wave. I was relatively unknown, the youngest competitor, up against the legendary Hawaiian surfers, and competing with my back to the wave, which back then was a fundamental disadvantage. I stood on the beach with my dad after the final ended, nervously awaiting the judges' decision.

The results came over the PA system: "In first place: Shaun Tomson."

It was a massive upset of the established surfing hierarchy and the biggest win of my life.

I hugged my dad. Perhaps his original dream didn't come true (that ended on a beach in Durban), but he helped his son achieve his, on another beach, halfway around the world.

THE SAGE

Let's say that life is a great party to which you have been invited. Now you have to decide what you want to wear to the party. The first thing to remember is that you get to choose not only from your clothing wardrobe but also from your emotional wardrobe; you must decide what feelings you are going to pull from your closet and wear to life's party.

The choice of what you are going to wear in the moments you are given is a gift. Let's talk about how you choose to open that gift.

Scripture says, "This is the day the Lord gave me, and I will rejoice in it." And while that's powerful information, it still comes down to how you frame your day.

Despair and hope are options that each have their moments.

Being filled with despair is not necessarily a flaw. There is a time for despair in life. Sorrow has its place. Just don't put it in the driver's seat and forget who's driving.

Those in the military like to remind us that "hope is not a plan." And they're right. But from hope, a move to the positive can be planned. Absent of hope, you are already defeated in life. Bottom line: dare to hope; plan to work.

Again, think about what you are going to pull from your emotional closet. Despair is not designer clothing; nor is it meant to be worn every day. Hope, however, is a superhero cloak that on the tough days, and even on the easy days, can shield you from despair. Hope and despair are both equal opportunity clothing options in every closet.

SHAUN TOMSON AT OFF THE WALL, HAWAII

III

DOUBT & FAITH

CAPE DISAPPOINTMENT LIGHTHOUSE, WASHINGTON

THE SURFER

grew up a person of faith—there was a God, there were places of worship, there was order in the universe and God was good. I had a bar mitzvah while attending a Christian primary school and could recite the Lord's Prayer in Latin—*Pater noster . . .*

I graduated to a Jewish high school and, every morning, attended a prayer service in Hebrew. Girls on one side of the assembly hall and boys on the other—wearing yarmulkes, prayer shawls called tallits, and tefillin (small leather boxes containing scrolls with verses from the Torah strapped to the arm and above the forehead). Ancient languages and symbols compounded the feeling of divine order, religiosity, and being close to God—there was comfort in tradition and dogma and observance.

While my parents were believers in God, my dad seldom set foot in the synagogue. It was my mom who would drag us to shul on Friday night, Saturday morning, and every Jewish holiday. But both of my parents saw faith as a fundamental building block of life, and every conversation over the phone, with my mother or father, ended with them saying the same words: "God bless."

I got my faith from my mom and dad, just like they passed on their DNA into my bloodline. I always thought that faith was an indomitable part of my being—rock solid—impervious to any outside force.

Then my faith and my life crumbled upon itself.

On April 24, 2006, on a sparkling spring morning in Montecito, California, I received a call from my broken wife, Carla, in South Africa, telling me that our beautiful fifteen-year-old son, Mathew, had died, a victim of the dangerous Choking Game.

In an instant, my faith was swept away by a giant wave of doubt—as well as despair and anger.

And I, too, was swept away, adrift from my mooring, faithless.

I remember crying out, "God, how can you do this to me? I have been a good person!" There was no order in my universe; was there even a God? Are we all just particles in Brownian motion—moving randomly and haphazardly through life, atoms bumping and being bumped, no order, no logic, no meaning or purpose?

I was bereft and broken, rudderless.

And then I got my faith back in a blinding bolt of lightning. When you lose a loved one, it seems the light of their soul, their energy, their essence, their atomic core of vitality, does not disappear with death.

After the tragedy, as my wife and I were recovering from the terrible loss, we had a visit from a close friend. Tony, who had also lost a teenage son the year before, had been to see a friend who was a grief counselor and a swami, a gifted individual whose vision can reach beyond what she sees.

He said he had a message from Mathew, that he was okay. And with that, one bolt of lightning hit the building we were in, rocked it to its foundation. **One bolt**, one single bolt of light, out of a clear blue sky. Light. **Light**. That was my way forward from doubt back to faith.

I would sit in Temple David—my old synagogue in Durban, South Africa, where I had my bar mitzvah and where Carla and I were married—and reflect and pray. I would think about Mathew, and I could feel him with me.

I took my mom's advice about prayer. "God doesn't look around and think *She hasn't spoken to me in years; why is she asking for help now?* It's simply what you do during times like those. You ask for help, and it's a very good thing and you hope God is listening. There is no time limit on praying— anywhere, anytime, silently or loudly, sometimes or always. God is like a good friend or neighbor who you can call on at any time and he is always at home."

I would look at that light above the ark, the light that is above every ark and above every Torah. Ner Tamid, the eternal light. The light that cannot be extinguished. The light of faith, the light that is an embodiment of the goodness of the human spirit and our connectivity to the everlasting.

THE SAGE

No one can doubt that "doubt" has sometimes been given a bad name. Like many inmates in a penitentiary, doubt could be screaming, "I've been framed!" And how something is framed has a lot to do with how it's seen.

For example, you can doubt that you're going to get rich, but it's up to you whether you will live a rich life. The difference is the faith you have in yourself.

The mirror on faith and doubt depends on who is looking and how they're looking. You can have doubts about having faith, but faith, by definition, is seeing what can't be seen.

Anyone can paddle out into the ocean with doubts about getting a great wave, but a great surfer will wax their board with faith and drop doubt at the shore.

A person of faith is not someone without doubts; a person of faith is someone who doesn't put his or her doubts in charge. Doubt and faith are self-proclaimed defamations or affirmations. It just comes down to how you want to wallpaper your inner living room.

Doubt is an adhesive that can stick to anyone, but it will not hold you together. In fact, it promises that it won't.

Faith is how you bond with life, whether it's faith in God or in yourself. Faith is believing that the great wave destined for you is still out there. And in you!

BANZAI PIPELINE, HAWAII

IV

CONFUSION & CLARITY

SHAUN TOMSON AT WAIMEA BAY, HAWAII

THE SURFER

Families across the world are all facing stress, anxiety, and despair—negative emotional states and a negative perspective represented by the simple acronym S.A.D.

As the world starts closing down or opening up again, we will all be venturing into our own new frontier and these negative emotions will not simply disappear.

How do we reframe our perspective and change our attitude? How do we cut through the confusion of never-ending crisis control and find clarity?

Over the last decade, I have asked hundreds of thousands of people across the world to do a simple twenty-minute exercise of introspection, visualization, and action.

A way to reframe perspective and change attitude, a simple tool to focus and find clarity of purpose—and perhaps even find a new path.

We live in turbulent times to be sure, and every one of us lives in a challenging sea; our attitude towards those challenges defines who we are and how we live our lives.

I believe our attitude is the light that shines from our souls.

Our attitude about the present defines our future.

Our attitude about the future defines the present.

Our attitude defines how we see the world and how the world sees us.

Our attitude is the power that propels us, and others, on a journey from where we are to where we want to be.

It is a fundamental choice for all of us.

What is our attitude?

Positive or negative?

Optimistic or pessimistic?

Hope or despair?

Light or darkness?

Confusion or clarity?

It is a simple choice. It is a choice to be made by everyone and this choice can change us, change our lives, and change the world.

Here is the way to actualize attitude change—a Code to turn confusion into clarity.

Pick up a pen and a clean lined sheet of paper; give yourself about twenty minutes to write your Code.

Write twelve lines, each line beginning with *I will*.

These affirmations, these simple promises, serve as a window into the soul of humanity and represent our ultimate life purpose.

While every line, and every promise, may be unique, the life purpose of people across the world can be represented by two simple statements of absolute commitment, optimism, and positivity:

I will be better.

I will help others be better.

What are your twelve lines to give clarity to your life purpose?

NORTH SHORE, OAHU, HAWAII

THE SAGE

For many of us these days, there is the feeling that if you're not confused, you're not thinking clearly. But just to be clear about this: confusion is not how things are, but how you are. The world changes when you do. Or, to put a slight twist on it: you don't see things as they are but as you are.

And clarity is being clear about this.

There isn't a car on the road that doesn't have windshield wipers. Why? Because if you can't see the road clearly, you are an accident waiting to happen.

And how do you remedy this situation? By turning on your wipers and cleaning your windshield, your window to the world. If this metaphor sounds too simple, your windshield is filthy.

The choice between confusion and clarity requires a profound honesty. Anyone who says they are not confused occasionally has been so confused for so long that it's an addiction to the familiar and the rejection of honesty. And we all decide the lies we want to believe.

Anyone who believes that they have achieved clarity in all things is suffering from hubris, not insight.

A great surfer in life is not someone who is absent of confusion but rather someone who rides his or her confusion into clarity. Be clear with yourself on this! And enjoy the ride.

WAIMEA BAY, OAHU, HAWAII

SHAUN TOMSON AT BANZAI PIPELINE, HAWAII

V

GUILT &
FORGIVENESS

RELL SUNN, QUEEN OF MAKAHA, HAWAII

THE SURFER

At sixty miles per hour along the 101 Freeway, while driving north through beautiful Santa Barbara, you might miss it. As you bust out of the city limits and look right, up on a hill, with the Santa Ynez Mountains to the north and the Pacific Ocean to the south, is the Santa Barbara County Jail, a small squat building housing nine hundred inmates.

The jail is under the control of a local Santa Barbara legend, Sheriff Bill Brown. Part Wyatt Earp and part Doc Holliday, our lawman, his moustache, and his ten-gallon hat are popular fixtures in our small town, and he is a calming public figure whenever disaster strikes. I sat next to Bill at dinner one night and mentioned my work empowering organizations and schools though my Code Method.

He mentioned his primary focus at the jail is transformation rather than incarceration. His mission is to give the inmates support so he never sees them again. Recidivism is a big problem for jails, and the best antidote is education and upliftment.

Over the years, tens of thousands of people—families, employees, and friends—have intimately connected with each other through writing and then sharing their Code aloud—twelve lines, each line beginning with *I will*.

It is a simple yet powerful twenty-minute exercise that reveals who you are and who you want to be.

It is a way to find and define one's purpose.

In today's uncertain world, when we are all fearful and stressed, the Code is an insightful way to visualize a better future and commit towards realizing it.

The Code is a tool of hope, commitment, and shared values. Everyone writes poetry of the soul.

A dean of a famous Hawaiian school said people write in a particular language—"spirit language."

I was curious as to whether my simple process of introspection, visualization, commitment, and action might work with inmates, so I visited with a few groups, both men and women, all facing one year to life.

I spoke to the inmates for about an hour, and then each inmate completed their twenty-minute exercise and wrote their Code. After reading their Code out aloud, each inmate then selected their most resonant line.

Their words were inspiring and uplifting, words of power and purpose that soared beyond the prison's walls. I was inspired that everyone was committed to changing not only their life trajectory but that of others too. Their uplifting words were like a wave of contagion throughout the jail— positive emotional contagion, not the negative contagion that is oppressing and depressing so many around the world.

Their powerful words are a way forward for all of us.

A few days after my visit, I received a touching letter from Jessica, an inmate who had just been released. She agreed to share her words to inspire others.

"Hi Shaun,

You don't know me, but I was recently incarcerated for a very poor decision I made and you were a speaker there. At Santa Barbara County Jail. Anyway, I just wanted to thank you for your time there and how much of an impact it made on my life. A life Code I have for myself from that day I saw you has been "always do the next right thing." I just wanted to deeply thank you for speaking. You opened my eyes to many things in life. And I am so greatly thankful I was able to hear you speak before I got released. I'll never go back there. God bless you and your family. :)"

I have had the unique opportunity of reading and listening to hundreds of thousands of lines of people committing to a new path by writing their Code.

The process is one of introspection and visualization—a way of turning hope and faith into commitment and action.

Every line contains power, passion, and poetry—the beauty of the human spirit is revealed from the inside out in the form of short, simple promises.

While every line is different, our fundamental life mission is defined by two tributaries of the river of purpose. Every line of Code flows into these rivers and then becomes one:

I will be better.

I will help others be better.

The two most powerful lines of Code, of immediate life transformation, of helping others and oneself, too, are *I will forgive* and *I will forgive myself.*

Words have great power to heal sadness and division in our lives and the lives of others.

Words are the precursor to action and are the bridge between thought and actualization.

I felt privileged to listen to the inmates write and state their Codes—their twelve lines of absolute commitment to transformational change.

People want to be better.

People want to help others be better.

One way to be better and help others be better is to forgive.

Simply saying it out loud in a group setting—committing to forgiveness, absolutely and unequivocally—is an immediate lightening of a crushing load.

Guilt is a bitter cancer poisoning the heart, a burden that ties one to the past.

Forgiveness is a sword through the rope that binds one to the post of bitterness.

Forgiveness dispels darkness and extinguishes the hatred burning inside the soul.

Forgiveness is the light that shines ahead while guilt is the bleakness of blame.

When an individual writes *I will forgive*, they are taking the first transformational step towards finding a new path in life—leaving the darkness of the past behind and venturing forward into the future.

Try it:

I will forgive.

SANTA BARBARA, CALIFORNIA

THE SAGE

Sometimes dealing with certain concepts in life is like conversing at a masquerade party: you're unsure who you are talking with in earnest conversation.

Guilt is one of those concepts that can seem to belittle you, but guilt's real role in your life is simply a call to be attentive and honest with yourself.

Guilt's function is for you to turn and look at what you did and say, "Damn! I did that, and I won't do that again."

If you think forgiveness is God's work, you are right and you are wrong. Forgiveness is not only work done at higher levels; it also, and no less, is when you forgive you. Showing yourself mercy is not a fool's errand. Mercy is surely God's grace, but make it yours also. Showing grace is a graced state in life. Just as knowing you are blessed is also a blessing.

And here's where it gets very interesting. Your ability to be forgiving of others requires you to be self-forgiving. Until you can be square and clear with yourself and your faults, you will be pointing fingers at others. Only those who can be self-forgiving can be other-forgiving.

St. Augustine reminds us, "No saint without a past. No sinner without a future." Amen. And if you're a sinner or a surfer, denying how you screwed up on the last wave won't make the next ride any better.

If you call a child a fool for long enough you will be a prophet. Don't deny the worst in you. Admit it to yourself and move on. That's your work; pack a lunch pail and get on with the work. Or you will get stuck in the past while the best waves are still coming your way.

NORTH SHORE, OAHU, HAWAII

VI

ISOLATED &
CONNECTED

SHAUN TOMSON AT OFF THE WALL, HAWAII

THE SURFER

A number of years ago, Glenn Hening, a maverick environmentalist, began an initiative to solve an environmental problem at Rincon, one of the world's greatest waves, located on the county line between Santa Barbara and Ventura, California. The luxury homes that bordered the surfing spot were connected up to septic tanks, and when it rained, the water table rose and the sewage leached out into a river bisecting the break that fed into the ocean. Water quality declined and some surfers were getting sick. Getting the homes connected up to a modern sewer system to properly dispose of the waste would solve the problem.

The remedy would cost millions of dollars. Glenn thought the best strategy would be to highlight the problem to the public, so he invited a group of local officials, media, and students to the beach at Rincon to spread the word. He asked me to present the students with a gift so they would remember the day. I decided to give the students the gift of surfing—or rather, the fundamental lessons that surfing had taught me about life. In twenty minutes, I wrote twelve lines, each beginning with *I will*. I called what I had written the "Surfer's Code" and printed up one hundred laminated cards to give out on Rincon Beach.

The card has become a touchstone for me, and my simple words have been read by many people around the world and taken my life down a different path, from surfing to teaching about the core principles of life. I sometimes refer to the twelve basic lines in the Surfer's Code as the twelve principles of humanity: faith, gratitude, humility, courage, love, hope, empathy, resilience, self-discipline, imagination, integrity, and kindness.

Two of my favorite lines in the Surfer's Code are *I will watch out for other surfers after a big set* and *I will realize that all surfers are joined by one ocean.*

Many people, including some surfers, think that surfing is inherently a selfish sport. Ask any surfer and they will tell you that a wave is best ridden alone. At popular surfing beaches like Rincon, hundreds of surfers will gather on the best days to ride the waves. Overcrowded conditions are not pleasant—tempers can get short, and the danger level increases as more than one surfer rides the same wave.

However, riding waves alone also presents risks—you can catch as many waves as you want without worrying about anyone else, but a bad wipeout and a hit to the head can mean death by drowning if there is no one around to initiate a rescue.

Whenever I am in the surf, I have always felt a profound responsibility to watch for others in the water—if a big set of waves comes through and sweeps surfers away in its path, I always look back to see if everyone is okay—I suppose it comes from the expectation that if I got into trouble, someone would help me out too.

In the surf, even with people who do not know one

another, we are this little connected, waterborne community, floating out there together, on the same ocean, looking for that special wave.

In surfing, there is a balance between isolation and connectivity that is reflective of the dynamic tension of life—the struggle between self and selflessness, between love and loneliness.

Isolation is dangerous, in and out of the water, while in community, we find safety and purpose. In the time of dislocation and disconnection during the COVID-19 pandemic, suicides, drug overdoses, and domestic violence increased dramatically. Ken Duckworth, chief medical officer of the National Alliance for Mental Illness, stated, "There is a mental health wave to this pandemic."

How can we watch out for other surfers after a big set and stay connected in the vast ocean of life?

How can we end another's isolation?

Pick up the phone, send an email, stop by safely—simply make contact with someone who needs the community connection. You know who they are—a friend, a family member, or a business associate. By reaching out, you just might be saving a life.

THE SAGE

I f you are feeling isolated and alone, in some ways you probably are. But here is the balanced truth: We are all alone together.

At no moment in your life does anyone know for sure what you are thinking. And that's true for everyone. So the privacy that is yours is also something that the person standing next to you is also experiencing. Consequently, in our shared isolation is our shared community.

Think about it: when you are feeling alone, truly alone, you can be truly empathetic to another. Say hello!

The philosopher Martin Buber described the difference between isolation and community as the difference between living in an I–it relationship with the world and living in an I–thou relationship with the world.

The I–it frame means you treat others as objects and, in turn, are self-objectified and experience isolation. The I–thou frame means that you treat others as an extension of yourself and, in turn, experience the connection in community.

Evil is done by those who treat the world around them as objects. The waves heading your way on the best day are inviting you to know that you are part of the wave, you are at one with the wave. Now that's the way to profoundly catch a wave! And honor your connection to waves that will rise after you.

WASHINGTON STATE

MONTEREY, CALIFORNIA

VII

EXHAUSTED &
INSPIRED

HONOLUA BAY, MAUI, HAWAII

THE SURFER

There are a few simple words that define the essence of great surfing. While maneuvers and techniques have evolved over the last thirty years, the essential DNA of what constitutes truly great surfing is unchanged: speed, power, rhythm, aggression, style, and imagination. Eleven-time World Champion and the greatest surfer of all time, Kelly Slater, has all this, and also has that little extra chromosome of intuition, a knowingness, a prescient reactivity to the ebb and flow of the ocean. His wave selection is uncanny, inextricably linked to a connectivity and understanding of the ocean's energy.

Kelly has a special connection with Jeffreys Bay in South Africa, the world's longest, fastest wave—a connectivity unlike anyone I have ever seen. There is some sort of sublime, deeper relationship there, hidden beneath the surfing you see on the surface. He has an intuition about him, a connectedness to the environment, an enlightenment, a rare understanding of how he fits into the natural order of life, and it shines through him brightly.

He once told me about an experience he had during a final at the J-Bay Open surf contest when he was up against his greatest rival, Hawaiian Andy Irons—an experience when dolphins inspired and guided him to where he needed to be when he was exhausted . . .

"The first day I was ever here I saw dolphins. I saw a shark, whales, flamingos, all within just a few minutes. So that really struck me. It just seemed like a place that was so alive. So much happening, so much going on with the wildlife, and then, when you go out, you're just a part of that. I mean the closest I've ever been to whales has been here. There've been a lot of waves with dolphins too. In fact, in that epic final I had with Andy Irons in 2005, before I won, before my last wave, there were dolphins going back out. And I was so tired; I was so out of my mind, with just about two minutes left in the final. I was so tired, and I'd almost given up, just because physically I didn't have much strength left, and I said, 'Well, I'll just follow these dolphins.' And I paddled right behind the dolphins all the way back out. And it was something pretty magical, and it was the last thought I had before I got that wave, which won it for me with thirty-two seconds left.

"That's when you wonder what that deeper connection is to nature and stuff, because I literally just said, 'I'll just follow these dolphins.' I was thinking in my head, *they'll take me to the right place*. And they did."

CANNON BEACH, OREGON

THE SAGE

Exhaustion has two faces.

Exhaustion can be the emptiness of not being engaged with life, or the exhaustion of those who are always bored because they have not been present in an effort to do anything.

And exhaustion can be born from the unending effort to do something, make something, be someone. And that exhaustion can be inspiring.

To be inspired literally means to be filled with breath. So when you are exhausted from a hard run in pursuit of all that life offers, stop, catch your breath, and be inspired.

In Scripture, when God blows into the earth, the first man, Adam, is born. Adam is literally inspired by God.

But the only way you can take a breath is by releasing your breath. Adam's first breath, the gift from God, is exhaled and passed around, so we are all, even now, inspired and conspiring, breathing together, even now, God's first breath.

Honor the dignity of an exhaustion well-earned and you will be inspired.

And in the family of humanity know that we are all conspiring together, hoping to catch our breath, hoping to catch the next wave, hoping to remember that we are breathing the ancient spirituality of all every time we take a breath.

Breathe deeply and you won't drown in the shallows.

CANNON BEACH, OREGON

CALIFORNIA COAST

VIII

POWERLESS & EMPOWERED

NORTH SHORE, OAHU, HAWAII

THE SURFER

A study by Professor Ralph Keeney at Duke University concluded that twenty thousand of the thirty-five thousand people in the fifteen- to twenty-four-year-old age group who die every year in the US die from poor decisions. Kids die from motor vehicle accidents, illegal drugs, homicide, and suicide, but these deaths do not just happen involuntarily. Young people put themselves into these situations. Dying young or not dying is not accidental; it is a matter of choice. Twenty thousand deaths results in an awful army of broken hearts—forty thousand parents, eighty thousand grandparents, hundreds of thousands of brothers and sisters, aunts, uncles, friends. Over a short period of a few years, millions are affected with the terrible sadness of loss caused by one bad decision, one poor choice.

I know from personal experience of the terrible grief associated with the death of a child. In 2006, our beautiful boy Mathew made a rash decision, a terrible mistake that cost him his life at only fifteen. Kids at his school wore ties as part of their school uniforms, and after school one day, he tried something called the Choking Game and it killed him. One bad decision made on the spur of the moment, and my boy was gone. And my life and my wife's life were destroyed.

The pain of losing a child is beyond awful, indescribably dreadful, an unending sadness that stretches out endlessly with no horizon, no end point, an agonizing journey on a ship sailing to the dismal port of hopelessness and despair. When I thought of our loss and think of the other forty thousand parents who are faced with that same hard and painful journey, I knew that I had to do something. What to do? How can one person help or influence a generation far removed from where I am now in my life?

A number of years after my loss, I started to tell my story to community groups, corporations, schools, and universities—I speak about my journey from the dark back into the light, about finding hope amidst despair. I talk about how two hours before my son died, he read me a beautiful essay that eloquently described the surfing experience, and how some of the words he wrote have become a mantra for me—*the light shines ahead*—so powerful and so full of hope. I think speaking about my loss helped me as much as I hoped it would help others.

I speak to young people about the awesome responsibility they have to make positive choices, to not react instinctively and just be a little more contemplative. Above all, I stress to young people across the country and across the world: "A day will come when you are faced with a life-or-death decision—it might not be today, it might not be tomorrow, but that day will come. You might be by yourself, or you might be with friends, or you might be with people who you think are your friends but who are not really who you think they are. Your parents will not be there and, ultimately, it will be you and the decision, you and the choice, you and life, you and death."

I used to be a pro surfer, so by the time I get to this part of the talk, I have shown some video of huge waves and exciting wipeouts, and I usually have the audience's attention. I say, "Try to remember that a surfer guy once came to visit you and told you about his son's one bad decision, and the pain he had to endure that broke his life, and how easy it is for you to bring the same pain to the people you love."

I say, "Please do this one thing, one thing only," and I ask the kids to repeat it. *Think twice.* "What you gonna do?" *Think twice.* Kids would listen to my story and my impassioned plea to *think twice*, but there was no call to action, just a call for a reaction to a potentially deadly situation. When there is danger, *think twice*.

I knew in my heart that while we all have limited control over our circumstances, we have absolute control over our attitude and our choices. Attitude powers choice, but I had no idea how to inspire an attitude change—I was just telling my story, yet telling of the risks was not enough.

What was missing was a way to create an attitude change, a way to create a feeling of personal power, a way to harness peer pressure as a positive force. I knew there had to be an answer, a simple way to empower positive decisions, and that answer was given to me by a young girl about Mathew's age.

Anacapa is a small local school of eighty students in Santa Barbara, and the headmaster, Gordon Sichi, who I had met in the surf, asked me to tell my story to his students. I was talking about my first book, *Surfer's Code*, which was inspired by a card I handed out to a group of students at an environmental event—a card of twelve lessons that surfing has taught me about life and business, success and failure, happiness and despair.

While speaking, an idea formed and, on the spur of the moment, I asked the students to write their own Code—twelve lines, twelve promises to themselves, every line beginning with *I will*. I told them that the original Surfer's Code, which formed the basis for the book, took me about thirty minutes to write—twelve lines, 105 words, each line beginning with *I will*: *I will always paddle back out*, *I will take the drop with commitment*, etc. "But the *Surfer's Code* is my words. What about your Code? Write down your words—define your purpose, activate your own power, and find your own path."

After the students had time to write their own Codes, the headmaster sent me the answers. Out of the nearly one thousand lines I got back, the first was *I will always be myself*. Once I read that, I knew I had to write another book—I was inspired and compelled to do it. *I will always be myself* is an anthem for youth. Kids living life their own way—doing what they want and not what their friends want them to do—that statement, that simple promise, is like a vaccination against negative peer pressure.

So I wrote a new book and called it *The Code*. It came from a place of hope—every chapter begins with *I will*—the book is about the future—the sun will rise tomorrow and darkness will give way to light.

The light shines ahead, the words Mathew read to me two hours before he died, have become a mantra, a prayer for my heart and soul, a connection to him that transcends time, space, and physicality—it is a spirit-to-spirit connection—a spirit language.

When you lose a child and suffer, you receive knowledge and an understanding that you do not want, but you get it anyway and you live with it because that is what keeps you alive. I know that the light does shine ahead; I know that the sun will rise tomorrow. I know that life is not futile, that we are not simply particles in Brownian motion.

Writing is a cathartic experience. Contemplation and then bringing your thoughts to life in letters and words is a positive release of pain in some way. The knowledge that perhaps what you write might help someone is a motivation. The knowledge that what young people might write to help themselves and their friends is an even more powerful inducement to try to spread the word of positive choice.

I am hoping for two things with my outreach—one, that the words in my books and my talks empower young people to think twice about that big decision that can kill them, and two, that a young person somewhere, sometime, stops when he is confronted by that life-changing decision, thinks twice, and maybe saves his own life.

That is my personal mission, and my message is pure and from the heart—it is what I believe and what I stand for, but I'm only one person and my words don't reach that many. The

ultimate goal and my mission is for young people around the world to write their own Code—a fusion of core values and a vision of the future—twelve simple lines of hope and commitment, their promises to themselves.

I have received hundreds of thousands of lines of Code from young people, but one of the most poignant was *I will live another day*. Perhaps I can save a life with my mission, perhaps not, but I am doing it anyway. I believe that there is great power in a personal Code, and if young people start writing their Codes and sharing them and inspiring each other with their own promises of hope, they can create a wave of pure and positive energy that keeps circling the world, uplifting hundreds of thousands as they ride on its power.

BACKDOOR PIPELINE, HAWAII

THE SAGE

I t would be funny if it wasn't true that when you wake up feeling powerless is often when you can decide it's finally time to be self-empowering. The lesson? Don't confuse how you feel with who you are.

Feeling powerless can be the observant humility that you are not in charge. What you are in charge of is how you choose to conduct yourself. And in many ways, it is the only thing you are in charge of. An example? You're powerless over what waves come your way in life. But you're empowered to decide how you are going to face your waves, survive your waves, and ride your waves.

Of course there are times when you will feel powerless. And that's when you have to decide whether to throw yourself a pity party or throw yourself into the fray.

To paraphrase a great teacher, "When you can't change the world, you have to change you."

And that, my friend, is never small change.

At another altitude, feeling powerless can be the right time to hand God the keys and empower the Divine to watch over you, guide you, protect you, and forgive you. As time can testify, this is the empowerment of having faith in a higher power.

You don't have to use drugs to get high; prayer gets you high. You just have to stop doing the things that bring you down. Now that's self-empowering.

NORTH SHORE, OAHU, HAWAII

NORTH SHORE, OAHU, HAWAII

IX

DEFEATED & UNBREAKABLE

THREE TABLES, OAHU, HAWAII

THE SURFER

We all deal with the possibility of defeat on a daily basis; thankfully, defeat is not like death in mortal hand-to-hand combat. In ancient times, sword-smiths would heat swords to a high temperature to make the metal less brittle and more flexible in battle. One's perspective on winning and losing is often the determinant on ultimate success or failure. I have thought that defeat is a tempering process that makes us unbreakable. I had a great teacher . . .

In today's turbulent time, it is helpful to look at yesterday for good and honorable advice about character and integrity and how to handle defeat to make us unbreakable.

My late father, Ernest "Chony" Tomson, volunteered in World War II and spent his service as a tail gunner fighting in the South African Airforce, flying in American B-26 Marauders on bombing missions against the Axis forces in Germany and Italy.

When the war was over in 1945, he returned home and resumed a swimming career—he had been one of South Africa's top young swimmers and it was his dream to compete in the 1948 London Olympics. But a savage shark attack while surfing ended that dream.

However, my father never lost his deep love for the ocean and never lost his passion for competition—he imparted this love and passion on to me, his firstborn son, and my brother, Paul, and sister, Tracy.

I started to compete in surfing contests at a very young age, and the advice he gave me throughout my career as a pro surfer is still resonant for any athlete and for any leader.

No matter the result from the judges, no matter how close or unfair the decision, he would make sure that I accepted the result—immediately. As a former athlete, he was aware that today's loser can become tomorrow's winner only if there is an understanding and acceptance that defeat is the journey to victory. The way to deal with defeat is part of the tempering process to make one bend and not break.

Knowing my dad as I did, there was nothing anti-feminist in his advice:

"When you win, win like a gentleman. When you lose, lose like a man."

Australians have a great word for whiners and poor losers: whingers. Incessant complainers who, after a loss, feel they "wuz" robbed and whose ego is so vast they simply can't comprehend losing.

When an athlete is defeated, that is the time to toughen up and be tempered. After a loss, I would shake hands with the winner—give a good strong squeeze and let them know I was there—and think *I have been beaten today, but I will not be beaten tomorrow*.

If you don't accept the loss immediately and can't move past the acceptance of the defeat, your career is done.

Every athlete around the world has a career defined by numbers—a win or a loss is always defined by a score or a time or a distance—no matter which sport, it all comes down to numbers, and numbers are a hard, inescapable reality.

No matter which alternative reality one believes in, numbers are the bedrock of truth.

I competed in my first surfing event in 1967 and surfed in thousands of competitions, winning some and losing a lot more.

My wise father would say to me after the heat or the final was over, "Remember the decision is final. Those numbers are carved in stone and no amount of moaning or crying will ever change the result. By complaining, all you will do is humiliate yourself and your family. Accept the result and move on."

At the time, my father was teaching me a fundamental lesson about life: keep an even temper. At the time of disappointment and defeat, be accepting, humble, and optimistic.

"Temper" is a good word to describe the process of heating and cooling to make us unbreakable.

THE SAGE

The root of the word "defeat" is from the Old French and means to be "undone." And that is the feeling you have when you have been defeated; you feel undone, left open, vulnerable. Of course you don't have to be defeated to be vulnerable, and feeling vulnerable is not a defeat in life, but "defeated" also implies you have been in a battle and lost. But do you really think that you are going to win all your battles in life? And isn't the first lesson in going to fight for something that you may lose?

Just don't confuse letting go with giving up!

The major difference between being defeated and being unbreakable is the decision that "yes, I am broken, but I am not defeated. And I am unbreakable because I can distinguish between the two."

A broken bone heals stronger for having been broken. Defeat is a split in the road. You can take the turn to defeated or you can take the turn to bring it on.

No one ever won the gold in anything in life, work, or love who didn't, at some time, find themselves a little black and blue.

On life's journey, you will experience injury. But remember, it is the great who play injured.

SHAUN TOMSON AT OFF THE WALL, HAWAII

TEAHUPOO, TAHITI

X

HUBRIS & HUMILITY

SHAUN TOMSON AT SUNSET BEACH, HAWAII

THE SURFER

One of the greatest compliments a surfer can receive is that they are a charger, someone who rides large, dangerous waves with courage, bravado, and skill—although a go-for-it, gung-ho attitude is not more important than mastery, talent, and ability. Being a charger implies absolute confidence with a sprinkling of arrogance and hubris.

During my time as a pro surfer, the center of the surfing universe with the world's largest waves was the North Shore of Oahu in Hawaii, a seven-mile stretch of coast that was home to four legendary surfing breaks bookended by Haleiwa in the south and Sunset Beach in the north. In between were Waimea Bay and Banzai Pipeline.

This was surfing's big wave zone; early surfers from the golden age in the 1950s and '60s would describe the boards they rode in this zone as "guns," a term still used today. To ride the very biggest waves, some surfers would use "elephant guns."

All of these four locations were used as pro contest venues; each had their own unique character and challenges, and all of them were ridable only during certain swells and sizes. Winter storms in the North Pacific generated large swells that would travel across the ocean and come sweeping onto the coastline. Haleiwa was a high-performance wave, Pipeline was a challenging tube ride, and both were best on west swells between six and fifteen feet. Sunset was rideable up to eighteen feet on any swell and was the primary competition venue—it was the home of big wave performance surfing. Three of the breaks are very consistent and break on a variety of swells. Waimea Bay is the outlier.

Waimea Bay is one of the most beautiful bays in all of Hawaii—a golden sand beach at the mouth of a verdant valley, clear azure water surrounded on both sides by craggy volcanic rock, and during summer, a perfect place for swimming and snorkeling. Waimea can lie dormant like this for many months at a time until the winter swells start rolling in between November and February. Waimea Bay transforms from a placid bay and yacht anchor to one of the most dangerous places on the planet. Despite this, Waimea seldom becomes closed out (which is when the swell gets too big to ride).

I saw Waimea Bay for the first time during the largest swell ever to hit Hawaii that destroyed many beachfront homes on the shore—absolutely unrideable, monstrous waves.

I knew of the intimidating wave from watching legendary surf films by Bruce Brown and Bud Browne—the huge wipeout sequence when surfers would get cannonballed into space and then freefall into oblivion were always the highlight of any surfing film.

I had my first opportunity to ride the wave during the finals of the 1975 Smirnoff Pro, at the time one of the world's most prestigious events. I had just turned twenty and qualified for the six-man final in powerful twelve- to fifteen-foot surf at Sunset Beach. Then the swell closed out and Sunset become unrideable. The contest organizer, former world-champ Fred Hemmings, moved the contest to Waimea Bay.

I stood on the beach watching some of the largest waves I had ever seen detonate on the coral reef about three hundred yards out. The waves were so big, they looked to be breaking in slow motion, like huge watery mountains falling over and crashing down with incredible power and ferocity.

I knew I needed a specialized board—a big wave gun at least nine feet in length. I had brought a few boards over from South Africa and had been sponsored with a few more, but I had nothing in that range. I found a friend who agreed to lend me his orange nine-foot gun, and I paddled out with a group of the best surfers in the world. I was the only surfer never to have ridden the break and the only surfer on a borrowed board.

We paddled into the takeoff zone, the location where surfers paddle into the wave, and sat up on our boards waiting. Waves travel into shore in sets or groupings, anywhere from three to six waves at a time. We all expectantly looked out to the horizon for the next set, jockeying for position.

Surfers don't wait in an ordered group—there is a constant positioning and repositioning with the inside surfer, the surfer in the most dangerous spot, closest to the breaking portion of the wave, having right of way. There is a constant push by other surfers to get to the inside, to get the right of way, but sometimes one can end up too far inside and out of position. There are a lot of tactics in the lineup—where to sit and then which wave in the set to catch. Getting the first wave can be risky, because if you make a mistake and wipe out, you have to deal with the next waves landing on you while you are still struggling for breath, without your board, in midst of the impact zone.

The first set bent into the bay and I was determined to catch the first ride—I wanted to make my mark in the final and at Waimea Bay. Any fear or trepidation I had was brushed away with determination and aggression. The first wave came rolling in, a solid twenty, twenty-five feet.

I paddled over the edge, leapt to my feet on the monster, and looked out at what seemed like the whole world beneath me. In that brief moment, atop that giant wave, I felt extreme exaggerated confidence and thought it was going to be easy, like so many waves I had ridden before. The words "I got this" flickered through my mind—hubris in action.

The wave at Waimea comes out of thousands of feet of deep water and then, slowing as the reef gets shallower and reaches a depth of about 60 percent of its height, a twenty- to twenty-five-foot wave will break in twelve to eighteen feet of water. At Waimea, on takeoff, it gets extremely shallow, and this wave stood up vertically.

My board launched off the wave and I started to freefall, the board beneath me straining to keep my toes on the surface. I was out of control, dropping but still trying to land on the board. I thudded onto the deck of the board with such force that my legs buckled and I bounced off and across the surface, skipping like a stone. Above me, the entire Pacific Ocean converged into a mountain of water that detonated on the base of my spine, driving me with incredible force into the dark below. The impact was unlike anything I had experienced before or since.

Before the finals, a close friend and rival, Australian surf champion Ian Cairns, had said to me, "When you have a wipeout at Waimea and get hit by the wave, it is like being run over by a Mack truck."

He was wrong—the wave hit me so hard, it felt like getting run over by four Mack trucks.

I had every fragment of hubris knocked out of me, absolutely obliterated with the concussive force of the wave. Never again would I paddle into a wave and think "I got this." It was a humbled and changed individual who got washed into shore, clambered up on his surfboard, and began the long paddle back out to the break, thinking about the mortal danger that can result from hubris.

Over the years, I have come to know that in humility is quiet, internal strength. Humility is an honesty with oneself, a self-assessment based on truth, and a knowledge that you are who you are, while hubris is who you are not.

THE SAGE

Hubris will inevitably invite you onto life's dance floor and admire your moves, whether you can dance worth a damn or not.

Hubris is the imagined applause when there is no or not enough applause in your life. Or to think on this in another way, hubris is the canned applause on an old TV show where most of the audience and cast have long ago passed away.

What hubris is mostly saying is, "Sorry you don't feel highly enough about yourself. But don't worry, I'm here to tell you that you are the toughest guy in the bar or the most attractive woman in the room. Or vice versa!"

But while hubris can be a false witness, being too humble is also hubris. There is a story of a guy whose church gave him a medal for being the most humble in his church. The next Sunday, the guy wore the medal to church and they took it away from him.

True humility is not letting what you think you know stand in the way of what you might yet learn. True humility is not putting your expectations in charge but minimizing your ego's disappointments in life. Because what's good for your ego isn't always good for you, and expectation is often the highway to despair and repair.

You are not in charge of what the world delivers to your front door. You are in charge of your response. Respond, don't react.

When you paddle out past the breakwaters in life, you are not in charge of what wave will come or how it will break. What will break you is if you live your life thinking you're in charge.

Here's something to tell yourself and perhaps your children: when humility dates hubris, it might be the beginning of a beautiful relationship.

And I leave you with this: don't confuse feeling like less with being worth less.

Sometimes nothing is
a louder opinion than listening.

—NOAH BENSHEA

SHAUN TOMSON AT OFF THE WALL, HAWAII

PISMO BEACH PIER, CALIFORNIA

XI

STUCK &
LIBERATED

SHAUN TOMSON AT BANZAI PIPELINE, HAWAII

THE SURFER

Sometimes it feels like the world is closing in—one is being crushed down, unable to move forward or back, neither left nor right—imprisoned, stuck.

Sometimes the best way to figure out our next step out of the mud is by simply connecting with nature.

This connection does not necessarily mean expending physical energy like surfing, hiking, biking, running, sailing, or swimming—it might mean doing nothing, just being close to the natural world under the blue dome of sky.

Surfers spend most of their time during an average two-hour surf session doing nothing, waiting for a wave rather than surfing. A well-known ad from Instinct, an apparel company I founded many years ago, had the words, "Waiting for waves is O.K. Most people spend their lives waiting for nothing."

A ride on a surfboard is generally brief, no more than twenty seconds at your average surf break—a hundred-yard traverse from takeoff to kick out and then a paddleback to repeat the process. Most of the time we just sit astride our boards, partially submerged on a fiberglass-covered sculpture of polyurethane foam. The sets are seldom constant, so there are long moments when no waves are ridden, when we do nothing.

Surfing has exploded in popularity recently, so the days of being alone in the surf with one's thoughts are long gone.

I'll wait for my wave with a group of other surfers, all looking expectantly out towards the horizon for that next set.

Surfers don't wait in an ordered line like for a movie, but rather they wait within a fluid grouping, each surfer changing position to be in the best spot to catch the best wave that is expected to be coming just over the horizon. Some surfers sit far out, waiting specifically for the bigger waves, while others sit closer in towards the shore, able to pick off more small yet numerous waves. A quick glance from shore and one just sees a crowd of people astride boards, bobbing in an undulating ocean. But there is a lot that is unseen—an entire world of doing nothing, patient waiting and thinking . . .

While waiting for that next wave, in the cool water, my legs moving gently beneath me as I sit astride my board, balancing me on the undulations of the ocean, the push and pull of the tide, the currents from the wind and the incoming swell forcing energy through the ocean, pushing in and out or perpendicular to the coast, I connect with an unseen rhythm, the current of the universe, and it flows through me, balancing my internal and external thoughts—my immediate thoughts of the next wave and what I have to do to catch it, and my internal thoughts of how I might ride the wave and what I will do on that next ride.

I have always believed that no positive result or achievement happens randomly; success is a result firstly of introspection and visualization and secondly of positively directed energy towards the result. This is the essence of the

Surfer's Code program that I propagate throughout organizations and schools across the world. Sit and think, and then write your future as a simple twelve-line Code, each line beginning with *I will*. Thought, commitment, and then action.

With this quiet thought in nature comes liberation.

For some, this process of thinking and waiting before writing implies one is doing nothing, but the exact opposite is true. Doing nothing is the essential condition of quietude and stillness necessary for the tiny spark of inspiration to flame up into a commitment to action.

Doing nothing is more important than just doing.

And doing nothing in nature is more important than simply doing nothing.

And science backs it up.

Researcher David Strayer from the University of Utah Department of Psychology states, "We are seeing changes in the brain and changes in the body that suggest we are physically and mentally more healthy when we are interacting with nature."

I suppose all surfers are attuned to these invisible forces—in my homeland of South Africa, I could taste the wind and discern subtle changes in barometric pressure—I could feel that surf was coming, confirmed by slight visible shifts in nature, by cloud patterns, temperature shifts, and dew fall. With this connectivity to nature comes a keen sense of self awareness, an innate sense of how one fits into the mosaic of the universe, an intuitive understanding of cause and effect, and effect and cause.

By doing nothing, I become more connected to the present.

By doing nothing, I become more connected to myself.

By doing nothing, I become healthier.

By doing nothing, I become happier.

By doing nothing, I become better.

Connecting to nature in any way can teach us all volumes about ourselves, our lives, and, ultimately, our business endeavors. Connecting to nature helps us to be happier, reinvigorating our minds, souls, and bodies with fresh air and gratitude for the open sky and God's work. If we are quieter and more thoughtful and more engaged with nature, we will be better and our spirit will feel unstuck and liberated.

For me, connecting to nature while out in the surf forces me to slow down, stop, and wait, languidly drifting across the surface of water, thinking deeply on what is and what is yet to come . . .

SHAUN TOMSON AT BURLEIGH HEADS, AUSTRALIA

THE SAGE

Feeling stuck in life can be the result of circumstances or how you are dealing with circumstances. Too often we choose to do something that is negative but familiar over something that is healthy but new. And here's why:

Your brain is like a bowl of Jell-O. And all the information you receive forms canals that run across the Jell-O. But once those canals start forming, your brain wants to start sending any future info down the same canals. Your mind is physiologically habit-forming. So being stuck is familiar turf, and your mind likes to keep it that way.

Once you've made up your mind, your mind literally makes you. Consequently, liberation takes a commitment to not be stuck.

To get unstuck, you must write your own emancipation proclamation. Nobody can free you until you free yourself. Being stuck or being free is not a state of mind, but it begins with your state of mind.

Human beings are the only animals that will set a trap, bait the trap, and step into the trap. Stop and think about the traps you set for yourself, how you bait your trap to entice yourself, and what the urge is that makes your trap attractive. We all do this in some ways. And the way out demands you pay attention and give witness to yourself if you are not looking for the same outcome. In the same trap.

Okay, life-surfers, tuck this in your wet suit as you paddle out into the waves you will face: no one has ever been liberated who at some point has not felt stuck. Welcome to the human club.

And if you're still feeling a little lost, remember this: no one has ever found their way who has not felt lost.

SHAUN TOMSON AT OFF THE WALL, HAWAII

XII

FEAR & COURAGE

SHAUN TOMSON AT WAIMEA BAY, HAWAII

THE SURFER

Courage was a vital ingredient to my success as a pro surfer riding some of the world's most dangerous waves. Courage is not revealed by introspection and careful thought but by an absolute commitment to leaning forward into risk, an awareness of fear.

Fear of failure is what often holds us back from success, and as a surfer, I know that taking action, pushing forward with **absolute commitment**, is a way to find the courage we all possess to vaporize the fear that we all feel.

Courage is the antidote to fear, and courage is a learned skill, just like leadership is a learned skill. We are not born with courage, just like we are not born leaders. We learn about overcoming fear and finding courage not through thinking but through commitment and, ultimately, action.

I had just won the World Surfing Championship, the youngest surfer ever to do so, and beneath my feet was a surfboard nicknamed the Pink Banana, a revolutionary and innovative piece of equipment with extreme rocker or curve (hence the name) that had enabled me to ride differently, changing the technique from one of stylish survival to powerful and radical maneuvering. I was young and strong, and I felt invincible.

On this particular wave at the Banzai Pipeline, I made my descent with ease, confidently and comfortably anticipating the ride ahead. The wave started to break ahead of me, forming an oval cylinder of water, a shimmery cavern fifteen feet high and fifteen feet wide, composed of tons of cascading water detonating on the coral below.

Surfers now call this maneuver "backdooring" the section—riding into the tunnel of water from the wrong side, as the wave breaks over on itself, driving into the tube when the wave has already broken ahead of you.

Riding inside the tube is a remarkable existential experience, a moment when life comes into perfect focus, when the immediacy and urgency of the moment is tempered by a feeling of stillness, by an awareness that one is connected to the entire fabric of the universe, riding inside an absolutely silent and solitary tunnel of water, a sense that the past is slipping behind your shoulder, the present is beneath your feet, and the future is just ahead, out of reach, represented by a spinning, hypnotic, tumbling tunnel of water just ahead.

When I surfed at my very best, when my mind, body, and soul were in perfect congruence, I actually felt I could curve the wave to my will. It wasn't ego, but rather respect and humility, a realization that I was part of the fabric of time and space, connected with the energy of the wave, my psychic energy, and the planet's forces.

I drove forward on this wave at the Banzai Pipeline, speeding through the tube, *back-dooring* the massive section as the west and north swells converged. Ahead of me, the wall seemed to stretch out for a hundred yards and the wave threw out over my head like a magnificent, vaulted ceiling, a surfer's Sistine Chapel painted with the shimmers and glitters of water and sunlight.

The wave sped up and so did I, and up ahead, perhaps twenty feet in front of me, I noticed the water was a sinister black for a fifteen-yard stretch. I knew it was the black coral of death, craggy creases tangled together by lava flows and the slow buildup of coral over millennia. The tide was at its lowest, the protective covering of water over the reef at its shallowest and most dangerous. I knew I had to get across that deadly coral barrier; I knew I had to cross the black water to live and to escape into the light and the green water on the other side.

This wave felt different to anything I had ridden before, and I felt something different inside, a feeling I had never experienced before while riding a wave: primal fear—deep, dark, elemental dread. I had always banished fear once I caught a wave; it would vanish in the wind as I paddled over the edge of the wave. While riding, I never felt fear; I simply focused on the wave itself, trying to surf as radically and smoothly as I could while the wave changed ahead of me.

However, this wave was vastly different to anything I had ridden before, reality happening much slower, my consciousness experiencing the moment more acutely. I knew deep in my being that a wipeout over the shallow reef, on a wave of this magnitude, would be death, just like how one knows that stepping in front of a car on the freeway is death too.

"Oh God, please don't let me die," I pleaded as the huge wave broke around me while I was hurtling forward towards the deathly shallows. I had never asked for my life to be spared while riding a wave, never known such deep, primal, and lonely fear. I had to make it across that coral strip, the darkest fifteen yards I had ever seen.

Some have faith and some do not; some of us realize that order in the universe and the balanced perfection of nature did not arrive from the haphazard collision of particles in Brownian motion. Yes, I made the plea to my God, to the order in the universe, to not let me die.

I had two choices facing me, to be completed in slowly spinning milliseconds: one, bail out off the back of my board before I got to the shallow shoaling section of reef and perhaps survive, or two, risk everything and go for the light.

With my faith, my internal force, and my surfboard, I leaned forward, into the fear, leaned into the danger, and my board accelerated.

Behind me, the wave heaved and exploded, blasting out an explosive gasp of compressed air. I was shot forward by the stinging spray, like being shot out of the barrel of a gun, crossing the deadly ribbon of black coral at maximum velocity, and then burst out into the sunlight, to green water and soft sand, my heart pounding with excitement, stoked to the absolute core of my being.

My God was with me and my faith inspired me to lean forward into danger, lean forward into risk, lean forward to gain more speed, lean forward to cross the darkest of barriers, lean forward to have one of my greatest rides, and lean forward to forever know that to power into fear with absolute commitment and faith is to be the victor over fear.

Courage is not an absence of fear, but a keen awareness of it, an absolute knowledge of it, and a domination of it by moving towards it, by making a deliberate decision to lean in towards the fear, to break down the barrier, to cross the dark coral, or whatever that personally defined barrier limiting a personal breakthrough may be. Courage is also the realization that even when one leans in, with all one's focus and all one's physical and psychic energy, that may not be enough, and sometimes a call to God helps one find that extra power to cross over the dark and into the light.

THE SAGE

Let's have the courage to be honest about courage.

Courage is not the absence of fear but how we wrestle with our fears. Write that down in your mind's heart and keep it close.

Courage and fear are tides on every shore. Like every other tide, there are high and low moments. And like all tides, they are visitors. They come and go and come again. Don't be convinced of long-term living arrangements with either your fears or your courage.

Your intention to be or not be either fearful or courageous is interesting, but your intentions are not necessarily synchronous with life's intentions. No one on shore or on a surfboard knows what the next wave will bring. Or bring again. Or equally, what, without warning, in life will go flat.

While courage can be running up a hill under gunfire, most real courage happens on a private stage. It is a mother who doesn't reach for the vodka bottle in the closet at eleven in the morning. It is husband on a business trip in a hotel who doesn't accept the invite to a woman's room. It is a twelve-year-old boy who is called a coward but doesn't accept a challenge from a bully to climb a dangerous tower.

There is no courage that has not known fear, and there is no fear that does not dream of courage. And at some point we will all wake to one or the other. And often both in the same night.

Others seldom see your fears or your courage. What is important is that you do. And what you do.

You will inevitably know moments when you are quietly courageous or turn your life over to fear. Welcome to the human country club—members and non-members only.

Now find a comfortable chair and think about how you might handle the next moment differently. And in your life, that can make all the difference. The difference is you.

Pass the word to any adult or child
who fears failing or failing again:

Go for it.

Go for whatever
you have always thought
of doing or being.

And if you think you are
already a failure,
then you have already
achieved your fear.

So now there's nothing
holding you back.

Go for it!

—NOAH BENSHEA

LARRY BERTLEMANN, RENO ABELLIRA AND
EDDIE AIKAU AT SUNSET BEACH, HAWAII

WAIMEA BAY, OAHU, HAWAII

XIII

GIVING UP & LETTING GO

SHAUN TOMSON AT BANZAI PIPELINE, HAWAII

THE SURFER

Some years back, when I was trying to find a new way through life after losing my son, Mathew, a local psychologist, a Zen Buddhist, gave me some good advice: "Abandon all hope of fruition."

Thinking on it, I know that I have followed this on my path through life . . .

How did I find that road?

Over the years I have watched many parents interact with their children at the beach during surf contests or on the sports field. While I often admire the parents' involvement, sometimes it seems to be for the wrong reason—it is more about the parent than the child. A drive for success that overwhelms the passion the child has for the game and, eventually, creates a split between parent and child that results in the athlete quitting the sport.

I had a father who loved to see me succeed competitively and who would do anything in his power to help me, but it was never forceful or overbearing. Sure, there was sometimes gentle firmness, but I never had a feeling that while I was in the surf, my dad was on the beach directing me to achieve success for himself. All my father wanted me to do was do my best. There was nothing beyond that, and nothing more that he or I could control.

My career was very much a collaboration, but in the water, I made the decisions—it was never ever discussed, it was the foundation of the relationship—my father gave time, advice, love, and direction rather than orders, anger, and control. Control is the primary issue that causes the parent-child relationship to fray during a sports career.

There are no parenting lessons for dads, or at least there weren't back then, but he instinctively understood that what was best for me was for him to let go. My father knew that giving up control and letting go was the best course to follow.

In my last year of high school, the best surfers from all over South Africa traveled to Cape Town to compete for the State President's gold medal. Cape Town is one thousand miles from my hometown of Durban, so it was a long ride south from the subtropics to what felt like Antarctica. The venue for the event was a beautiful stretch of unspoiled windswept beach called Dunes.

Just prior to the event, I picked up a nasty stomach virus and spent a week in bed, vomiting and with a bad case of diarrhea. I was a skinny kid and in a few days lost over ten pounds—I was weak and lethargic, but after a visit from my cousin Mark Awerbuch, who was completing his residency at Groote Schuur, and a prescription of Lomotil, I was back on the road to recovery and started to feel better.

Once I managed to get out of bed, my dad asked me whether I wanted to compete. I could feel that he preferred me not to, but the decision was my own.

The surf was beautiful for the event—four- to six-foot waves, breaking left, running down the beach.

I was weak and spent all the heats in a state of exhaustion— I paddled slowly but picked my waves with great care, eventually making it through to the finals. My toughest competition was Ant Brodowicz, an explosive goofy foot surfer from Margate. I had resigned myself to not aim for the win—my objective was to simply be out there, for myself and for my dad. It wasn't that I gave up, but I let go.

During the final, Ant and I both finished off some good rides, but once it was over, I had no idea whether I had won or not. I walked back to the car to get changed into dry clothes, then started the long walk back to the contest site, walking atop the dunes, stepping through the crisp white Cape sands that squeak with every footstep.

Halfway back across the expanse of dunes, I could see my dad coming towards me. I knew he was proud of my effort—I was proud of myself. We came together, father and son, and he put his arms around my shoulders and started crying. "You won," he said. "You won." And he started crying. It was the only time I ever saw my dad cry after a contest result.

I had yet to win a professional surfing event, and a career in surfing was years away. I eventually went on to win nineteen major professional events, at times the youngest to win while at others the oldest. I enjoyed many of the wins with my father—he was on the beach with me in Hawaii when, at twenty years old, I won the world's most prestigious event: the Pipeline Masters.

Most of my records have since been broken and many of the wins I can't clearly remember. But I remember that win, with my father atop a sand dune in Cape Town, a moment of pure love and joy—a win that was based on giving up and letting go, and a father-son relationship that was built on the same foundation.

CANNON BEACH, OREGON

THE SAGE

For too many of us, the operating instructions that were bred into us, the way we were raised or the culture we were raised in, programmed us to face life with an agenda of "approach and conquer." The consequence of this attitude diminishingly frames our life experience as a win-or-lose experience. To this understanding, you can also add this truth: how you win or lose is more important than if you win or lose.

Certainly we have all witnessed "winners" who are "losers," as well as those whose gallantry is in how they struggled in the face of events' crushing waves.

In the face of this false conflict as an approach to life, let us now look at two other of life's battle maneuvers. Let us look at the distinction between giving up and letting go.

Giving up is not a defeat if you have given your all. Life is too short to spend any amount of time needing to be right.

Letting go is not defeat if you do so because it serves you rather than because you want to be right. And nothing is more a waste of time in your life than always needing to be right.

Learning when to let go is not giving up, but it can give you a chance to catch the next wave that will carry you on and lift you higher yet.

Empty yourself of what does not serve you. Nothing attracts everything like needing nothing.

Whether you find
gain in loss
or loss in gain
depends on how
you play your game.

Now or then
the game's the same.

—NOAH BENSHEA

NEW SOUTH WALES, AUSTRALIA

XIV

FRAILTY & RESILIENCE

NORTH SHORE, OAHU, HAWAII

THE SURFER

Billions of people around the world are struggling to find reserves of resilience during these troubled times of pandemic, economic uncertainty, and social dislocation. We have become beaten down—we have become frail.

Instead of bending, we feel like breaking . . .

How can one find the strength and internal fortitude to combat the S.A.D. mindset of stress, anxiety, and despair?

How can one become strong again?

Who can one ask for help?

Who can help?

Ask God by sending out a prayer.

Here is some wisdom about prayer from my ninety-year-old mother, Marie, who endured thirty-four hundred air raids during World War II while living on the island of Malta—the most heavily bombed territory on Earth. Her family suffered two direct hits from German and Italian bombs, their home destroyed around them, but somehow she survived and lived life with an indomitable spirit of love, hope, optimism, and resilience.

"God doesn't look around and think *She hasn't spoken to me in years; why is she asking for help now?*

"It's simply what you do during times like those. You ask for help, and it's a very good thing and you hope God is listening.

"There is no time limit on praying—anywhere, anytime, silently or loudly, sometimes or always.

"God is like a good friend or neighbor who you can call on at any time and he is always at home."

When you feel frail and about to break, send out a prayer for yourself, and send out a prayer for someone else too.

Someone else who epitomizes resilience is the iconic South African leader Nelson Mandela. Shortly after retiring from the professional surfing tour in 1990, I watched Nelson Mandela walk out of prison as a free man after twenty-seven years in jail—a symbol of freedom, forgiveness, discipline, dedication, and righteousness. And especially resilience.

Four years later, he cast his vote for democracy at Ohlange High School—the first school founded by a black South African, John Dube. Built in my home province of KwaZulu-Natal in 1900, it is one of South Africa's most iconic schools.

John Dube based the school on Tuskegee University in the US and focused his teachings on self-reliance and resilience. For the name of the school, he chose a Zulu word that means both "reed" and "new growth."

John Dube ultimately became the first president of the African National Conference, South Africa's most important political party.

In 1994, in South Africa's first democratic election, Nelson Mandela cast his first vote at Ohlange School and laid a wreath at Dube's grave, stating, "Mr. President, I have come to report to you that South Africa is now free."

Almost twenty-five years later, I was honored to talk about the Surfer's Code at this historical school. The following week,

Principal Justice Mtshali (who later asked me to come to the school every month!) sent me an inspiring video of his young daughter who had taken the Code program into her primary school. Seven-year-old Anele, in first grade, was busy teaching sixth graders, continuing her family's teaching tradition, and taking a little piece of me with her on the journey.

Whenever I think of that school and its place in South African history and culture, and how its people were initially downtrodden and disadvantaged, I think of a vast meadow of reeds being pushed down as fierce winds and storms thunder across the African veld and then bouncing back upwards with the power of resilience and new growth—bent but never broken.

THE SAGE

The poet-philosopher Blaise Pascal reminds us, "Man is only a reed, the weakest in nature, but he is a reed that thinks."

So acknowledging we are all frail, let us think on this. A frail, hollow reed can be turned into a fluted instrument that makes the most beautiful music. The frail innocence of a child in a manger is embraced globally as divine. Frailty is not a flaw. It is a state of being. But don't confuse being frail with being broken.

Resilience doesn't mean you have not been broken. Resilience is what happens after you feel broken. A broken leaf can sail downstream. A broken bone heals stronger for having been broken.

Resilience is not a physical state. Resilience is a state of mind and where your spirit chooses to call home.

Perhaps think of frailty and resilience as a law firm. When you call their number, the voice that answers asks to whom you wish to be connected, frailty or resilience.

Frailty and resilience reside in all offices of the human experience. In your life, learn to have frailty and resilience consult with each other and ally to be cross-supportive. After all, you may be a reed, among the weakest thing in nature, but you are a reed that thinks.

Jacob was a hollow reed,
but the breath of God
blew through him,
made music of him.

—*NOAH BENSHEA*, JACOB THE BAKER

SHAUN TOMSON AT BANZAI PIPELINE, HAWAII

PESSIMISM & OPTIMISM

TERI MELANSON AT ROCKY POINT, HAWAII

THE SURFER

Life is uncertain and unpredictable, and surfers know this better than most.

When I decide to go surfing, I am never really sure of what I am going to get, if anything, but I go anyway. Why do I get up in the dark, leave behind my wife and child, and head out in the cold? Optimism is this implacable hope that I will get what I need in the surf even though success is decidedly uncertain.

Surfing can't be perfectly planned out like a game of golf, tennis, baseball, or basketball.

We can't say let's meet at 3 p.m. and be done by 5.

Waves don't run to a schedule and neither does the wind, which often turns the wrong way just as you arrive. But as surfers, we go anyway. There is an essential optimism associated with a life built around the ever-changing ocean—a fundamental hopefulness that out there, amidst the vast sea and amongst the other surfers, the right wave will come. And there is also this perspective and knowledge that no matter what, there will always be another wave.

From a life spent in the surf, optimism swells in my heart like the ocean at high tide.

There is that old adage that an optimist sees a glass of water as half full rather than half empty, a simple analysis of one's perspective on life: full or empty. But I think optimism is not simply a way of looking at life. Optimism is a gratefulness about the present and a confident hopefulness about a better future.

While a pessimist might worry and fret over possible failure, an optimist is focused on a successful outcome. To take the glass and liquid metaphor a little further, to the pessimist, that may be the last glass and the only water, while the optimist knows that there will always be another glass and more water. Optimism is the fuel that drives us forward while pessimism is the fear holding us back.

In my hometown of Durban, South Africa, our apartment on the tenth floor faced east, just across the street from the beach, overlooking the sea from on high, a view that stretched out endlessly across the Indian Ocean, under the blue curved dome of sky. If I shot off an arrow, with an infinite supply of power, it would glide across the sea and, in a straight shot, come down on the first landfall in Perth, Australia, 4,717 miles away.

Each morning, I would make my way across the narrow strip of beach and dive into the warm water as the blood-orange African sun would explode up out of the horizon, bathing me in its light and warmth. Paddling out toward that sun was how I started most days. If I close my eyes right now, I can be transported back to that feeling of happiness and hope, that optimism that the future was just ahead of me and I was confidently moving in a good direction towards the light.

NORTH SHORE, OAHU, HAWAII

THE SAGE

An optimist is someone who will see opportunity in every difficulty, and a pessimist is someone who will see difficulty in every opportunity.

If this clears things up, good. But with language, caution is advisable.

While language can serve us, it can also enslave our intentions as we understand them.

For example, pessimism doesn't mean you examine what can happen with caution, nor is it what is too often misconstrued as the weighing of what can happen.

Pessimism is when you assume that anything that can go wrong will go wrong, and you are just waiting for the universe to catch up with the despair you are inviting into action by your forethought of the negative.

Pessimism is being wed to why the hell should I try anyway? Pessimism is tying an anchor to your surfboard before you paddle out in life.

Optimism is not the balance to pessimism. Optimism doesn't operate out of that balance notion.

Optimism's first rule is that anxiety won't improve the future. Optimism takes an oath that the positive will come my way, and if it doesn't, it will soon.

An optimist who doesn't see things come his or her way says "I'm just not being optimistic enough" or "the universe still hasn't gotten the message so I've got to keep going and send out the positive vibe again."

A pessimist is always sure that something somewhere will go wrong. And asks, "Why the hell should I pack a parachute that I know won't open?"

An optimist packs a parachute but is sure he or she won't need it. And thinks, "Besides, if the parachute is needed and doesn't open, God will be there to catch me."

In some way, we all pack a little of the pessimist and a little of the optimist into the luggage on our journey. Or have our luggage packed by faith, family, or experience.

Anyone who has ever surfed knows the talent is in more than how you catch the waves in life, it's how you lean when the wave is under you. Lean into the optimism in life, and enjoy the ride!

SHAUN TOMSON AT BACKDOOR PIPELINE, HAWAII

XVI

TENTATIVE &
TENACIOUS

SHAUN TOMSON AT ROCKY POINT, HAWAII

THE SURFER

T he decision of who will be our life partner is one of the most important decisions one shall ever make. Whether we are tentative or tenacious in making that decision will determine our future . . .

Each year, the Durban Designer Collection was put on in my hometown of Durban, South Africa, a grand event held at the even grander City Hall, a dramatically beautiful building designed by architect Stanley Hudson in the Neo-Baroque style, an architectural vestige of the British empire in South Africa. People would often joke about my home province (in what is now called KwaZulu-Natal) as "the last outpost of the British empire in Africa," from the days when imperialist Cecil John Rhodes tried to paint the map of Africa British red with the building of a railroad from Cape Town to Cairo.

My brother, Paul, had recently flown out from the US to help me open Surfbeat, a surf shop near the beach, an offshoot of a store we had started together in Los Angeles. Because of my connection with fashion through Instinct, a brand I had started a number of years before, I thought we could both have a fun evening checking out the creativity of the Durban designers—and the beautiful girls too.

It was an enjoyable evening, models and children coming out onto the catwalk and parading up and down in the latest and greatest designs. I don't remember that much of the show itself except there was a large and enthusiastic crowd.

At intermission, we all congregated together in the lobby and I looked over and caught the eye of one of the designers who had just presented her collection, Carla Winnick. *Kaboom!* Just that one glance was like a bolt of lightning through my heart—the attraction was instantaneous and absolutely compelling—at least from my side it was . . .

I had known Carla when she was a child—her mother, Vivienne, and my mother, Marie, had been best friends before they both got married. While Carla was born in South Africa, her family moved to London when she was very young and then returned to South Africa a few years later. On arrival, they stayed with us in our apartment for a few months while they found a place to stay.

So the family went back a long way, but I hadn't had much contact with Carla since those early days as children— she moved in a different circle—she had become a top horse rider and jumper, and fashion and travel were her life. I joke that Carla moved in the polo set and I moved in the surf set and the two just never met—the field and the waves were a long way apart; in fact, chukkas and tubes were a world apart.

At the time, I was only in South Africa for a short period—I had recently won a pro contest in Cape Town, and the European leg of the professional surf circuit was about to start. I would spend around nine months at a time on the road, and my life was surf and travel. If I was to meet Carla again, there was no time to be tentative or take a leisurely approach. It was time for action!

I walked over and said hi and my life changed right there, right then. I knew this was the girl for me, a reaffirmation of that electricity I had felt across the crowded room. I could feel that she could be my life partner. Her look, her style, her beauty, warmth, scent, and composure enveloped me—she had a confidence, elegance, and fluidity that was utterly compelling and absorbing.

After speaking for a brief time amidst the crowd, I walked back to my brother and said, "I'm going to marry that girl."

The next day I picked up the phone to arrange a date for that night—I was in a hurry—I was going to be leaving town and if this grand plan was going to happen, it had to happen quickly!

Carla was soft-spoken and gentle but couldn't make it that night. Perhaps in a few days. I couldn't remember when I had last been turned down for a date and it was a bit of a sting. So I called back the next day and the answer was the same—call again when the timing might be better. When I called on the third day, I was finally able to wrangle our first date, which flowed into a love affair, a life together on the pro tour, marriage, and children.

I sometimes think how different my life could have been if I had behaved differently during that moment of decision and that time of gentle rejection. I could have been tentative in my first approach and Carla would have gone on her life path and I on mine, and we would never have intersected. I was about to leave on my world tour while Carla had her design career in South Africa.

I could have not called back after the first no and then the second—I could have let my ego get in the way and decide to simply move on.

But I didn't . . .

I have come to realize that one must take action to take charge of one's destiny—being tentative is like being stuck in the valley of indecision, between the peaks of action and inaction. You gotta cross that valley of indecision, where being tentative means staying stuck.

Initially I got knocked back by the woman who ended up being the love of my life, but I kept going. I was not going to be stopped; I was going to do everything in my power to actualize what I felt was my destiny.

Being tenacious is the bridge between action and inaction—it is the way forward in sport, business, and love too.

SHAUN TOMSON AT OFF THE WALL, HAWAII

THE SAGE

Tentative" and "tenacious" are terms whose real meaning is defined by the degree you engage with tentativeness and tenaciousness.

Tentative, to be cautious, is okay and sometimes wise right up until the time it isn't. No one ever caught and rode life's waves if they only planned on sticking their toe in the water. In life and love, you sometimes have to throw yourself in or you get thrown out of the opportunity.

Another way to know this is when the person or job of your dreams says, "Love me with abandon or I will abandon you!"

Tenacious, highly regarded as the stick-to-it effort in life, raises the issue of when abandoning an effort is the difference between giving up and letting go. Letting go says, "I'm not giving up. I'm going back out. Again. And again. Like the waves in the ocean and life, I'll keep coming. And tenacity is my surfboard. How often I get thrown off is irrelevant to my intention."

Most of us are too often self-congratulating and too often self-flogging. And being tentative or tenacious about either of these character manifestations can be a service or a disservice.

Hold tightly to the best in you and stop whipping yourself when you are less.

Here is the sum of it: your work in this life is not what you do but rather who you are.

So being tentative and/or tenacious really requires you to pay attention and moderate your commitment to either. Be cautious right up until the time you have to throw caution to the wind.

If this advice sounds contradictory, so is life. And the balance in life is often in the contradiction. That's the night and day of it. And, says mortality, the life and death of it.

When my son was young and someone asked him what his father did, he replied, "My father types." And I still type. But no book can give you the answer as to when it is the right time for you to do one thing or another.

If you think that experience will alleviate your dilemmas, here's my typed reply: Experience is a good teacher, but the tuition is your life. Be both tentative and tenacious about how much you will spend on that tuition.

CARMEL, CALIFORNIA

XVII

UNCERTAIN & COMMITTED

SHAUN TOMSON AT OFF THE WALL, HAWAII

THE SURFER

As a surfer, I have spent tens of thousands of hours floating on the surface of the sea.

The ocean is a place of uncertainty. Under the curved blue dome of sky, I have gazed optimistically toward the horizon looking for the unseen, trying to discern exactly where and when to catch the next wave, that band of energy created from the friction between wind and water. Like the invisible energy that ultimately shows itself in the form of a wave, our life purpose is invisible, too, and only reveals itself in the form of the decisions we make.

When that wave eventually comes, the only way to catch it is with absolute commitment. There can be no uncertainty or equivocation.

For a brief moment, as a surfer paddles for the wave, one has to match the wave's speed. Surfers call this the "takeoff," the moment when one feels the wave's power and the wave's energy is matched by the forward momentum of the paddling surfer. As the wave rises up to its highest and most powerful, the surfer plunges over the edge and leaps to his feet, in one fast and fluid moment, to begin the ride. Taking off requires a split-second decision; the surfer must absolutely and unequivocally commit to the takeoff, be committed to taking the drop into the steepest part of the wave.

Underlying all positive decisions, in and out of the surf, is commitment, our internal personal power that drives us to action. Commitment and purpose are twin forces that provide us the certainty to know that when the next wave comes, we will take off and not sit and wait endlessly, paralyzed by uncertainty, by what might happen rather than what we will make happen.

Finding purpose need not be complicated; it can be found through a simple twenty-minute process of introspection, visualization, and commitment called the Code Method.

Pick up a pen, give yourself twenty minutes of quiet time, and write twelve lines, each beginning with *I will*. This Code is a way to find, refine, and define one's purpose. The Code is twelve lines of absolute commitment.

Commitment is a way to break through the bonds of uncertainty, a covenant with ourselves, a promise to be better and make others better, a call to action.

Commitment to a better life is not difficult, and it starts with two simple words: *I will*.

SHAUN TOMSON AT SUNSET BEACH, HAWAII

THE SAGE

I f you are uncertain about making commitments or are committed to being uncertain about anything, you are in the company of everyone at some point in time. You can be certain of that.

If you are feeling uncertain about your life and the events in your life, you might be feeling vulnerable, but you might just be an honest witness. And regardless of what you may feel is on shaky ground, you need to remember that all personal transformation requires you to be an honest witness to what you are feeling and to not confuse what you are feeling with who you are.

The tides of uncertainty and certainty don't come with a tide chart. What they do come with is their own certainty. They roll in and out of every life. So don't confuse the moment with what the next moment will bring. Everything is pending. Stay tuned.

Being committed means you care. About something or someone. It doesn't mean you are in control of what that caring will bring. Don't confuse commitment with control.

Commitment is engagement, not clinging. In clinging is suffering. In commitment is participation with caring. It is saying, "I am going to fully engage this wave but acknowledge that I am not the wave nor the wave's intention."

Commitment in relationship is a commitment to guard your own solitude. Only those who can be committed to their own company can be good company to others.

Society sometimes uses the term "committed" when someone is incarcerated for mental health concerns or criminal conviction. And yet you don't have to be convicted in a court of law to be confined to doing time in you. Just keep in mind that your parole usually requires you to be self-pardoning.

There are waves rising in every sea, in every life, in every moment. Be committed to knowing this and knowing who you are when that wave rises under you and invites you to know your ride as the ride of a lifetime.

Are there dragons in life? Yes, but be clear with yourself that you've had your time as your dragon, and now you are a knight who is committed to the hero's identity.

Your mind will be self-reminding that life is uncertain, and yet, embrace your uncertainty with commitment, for that is the hero's oath.

PFEIFFER BEACH, BIG SUR, CALIFORNIA

XVIII

PRIVILEGE & GRATITUDE

BACKDOOR PIPELINE, HAWAII

THE SURFER

rivilege is a feeling of entitlement, a sense that the world owes you a debt to be repaid.

Privilege implies exclusivity and selfishness.

Gratitude is thankfulness for what one has, not for what is due.

While *I love you* may be the most beautiful statement in any language, *thank you* comes a close second. Gratitude is the sacred oil that enables human interaction. Gratitude is a sign of respect and humility. Gratitude has great power and is built on acceptance, not acquiescence.

During my professional surfing career, I spent many months in Japan, traveling and competing across the country. This was some time ago, when foreigners were rarities—children in their black school uniforms would stare, point, and giggle at the hairy foreign giants on the subway. I had read many books on Japanese culture, tradition, and history and admired the simple courtesy each person showed for one another while living and working in very tight and cramped quarters.

When one would meet a Japanese businessperson for the first time, there was always a structured exchange of business cards—a simple ritual of gratitude, respect, and courtesy. One would look the other person in the eye, hand over the card with both hands, and bow, then repeat the process to receive the other's card. It was both giving and receiving, a ritual of both gratitude and honor. No matter the relative status of the people meeting, whether one was a new employee or a CEO, there was no superiority or privilege associated with the exchange. The bow of the head showed both respect for the other and gratitude for the interaction. The process was an elaborately stylized form of a simple thank you for meeting, a more nuanced version of the westernized crushing hand-shake model.

It was interesting to see this process of gratitude and honor in action, in the surf . . .

It was an early morning in an area called Shogun, and surfers were practicing just prior to the start of one of Japan's largest pro events. The surf was very small, around two to three feet in height, and breaking close to the shore. Just before events, the pressure level rises and hot tempers can explode very quickly.

I was walking out into the surf and noticed two surfers, a Hawaiian and an Australian, riding towards one another on the same wave. This often happens in crowded conditions, and one surfer has to give way. Well, neither surfer wanted to yield to the other, and they both collided and wiped out, both falling underwater.

The wave passed by and both surfers stood up in the waist-deep water and started screaming at each other, then started swinging. It was more slapping and shouting than real violence, but it was an ugly scene, not a great representation of pro surfing and the spirit of the lifestyle.

On the very next wave, two local Japanese surfers did exactly the same thing, rode towards each other, crashed, and wiped out. As I watched the drama unfold, I thought to myself, *What am I going to see now? Is this going to be a karate conflict, a scene from a Bruce Lee movie?*

The two surfers stood up in the shallow water, moved towards each other, looked at one another, bowed deeply, got on their boards, and paddled away . . .

A simple expression of gratitude, like a simple "thank you" or subtle bow, can be a salve for internal and external conflict. Gratitude is not acquiescence, but true power associated with self-esteem and self-worth. *I value myself, but I see you, and I value you too.*

Being grateful and showing gratitude by saying "thank you" is like a magical balm that can calm a turbulent soul. Gratitude is respect for others and, equally importantly, respect for oneself.

THE SAGE

One of the most common and yet amazing things to witness is how often people who are privileged don't witness their privilege. And while it would be easy to lay a condemning attitude on this, the truth is that almost all of us are blind at some point to not seeing what we've been looking at for a long time. Familiarity breeds its own blindness.

If on your journey you have been blessed by a lot of green lights, it may be your turn to put your foot on the brakes and witness, "Hey, I'm blessed." Why? Because to count your blessings is also a blessing!

Gratitude is a grace. When you pause and are grateful for what has landed in your hands, there is a place for the grace of God to also land.

Now, you may think, "Well, I've worked hard and deserve what I have received." And there may be truth to your labors.

But do you doubt for a moment that there are people who have worked just as hard, or harder, for longer and still don't have a roof over their head or food to feed their children?

So, get over it. You are lucky. But what you may call "lucky" is in fact privilege divinely given. And if you want the stars in your favor to turn dark, take them for granted.

There is an old joke: "Where was Moses when the lights went out? In the dark!" Whoever you are, great or small, if you turn off your lights to gratitude, you will be in the dark.

There is no surfer who paddles out and presumes the privilege of only getting the best waves. They may paddle out with a positive attitude, but nothing serves a better attitude than gratitude. Be in gratitude for the waves that break your way in life.

You may be asking, "Well, what about when the waves in life knock me off my board?" In that moment, here's the gratitude meditation: "I am alive. I am on a beach. I can swim out again."

Here's the point: Each of us, including you, at some point leaves our gratitude at home when we head out the door. And then we forget that we have a door, and a roof, and somebody under that roof who loves us. And a divinity in the heavens who, according to all the Abrahamic religions—Judaism, Christianity, Islam—loved us enough to create us.

God—however you envision God—is omnipotent. So God could not be forced to do anything God didn't want to do. And that means? And that means birth is a sign that God was in gratitude to bear us. To have our company.

And what does that leave you? It leaves you every reason under the sun to be grateful. And you are privileged to be grateful. And me too. Amen.

CANNON BEACH, OREGON

A FINAL PERSPECTIVE

PORTLAND, MAINE

THE SURFER

It had been a number of years since I had been back to my homeland of South Africa. The night I arrived, an old friend heard I was back in town and phoned to take me surfing. He said he would take me to a wave that seldom broke, a rare break that he knew I had never surfed before. I knew straight away if I'd never ridden it, it wasn't going to have shark nets, and I would have to confront my ever-present fear of sharks. I had always had a deep fear of sharks—I suppose it came from knowing that if a shark got my dad, one could get me too.

Early in the morning, we drove down the highway that ran along the coastline and pulled off the side of the road near a break I had driven by many times but always on the way to somewhere else. I'd seen good-looking waves there before, but it always looked a little bit "sharky". We looked up the point in the half-light and could see solid six-foot-high sets rifling down the beach towards us.

We quickly changed into our wetsuits, waxed our boards, and walked down the long beach together, crunching through the coarse granular sand. I looked right, across a beautiful, lush valley, my face feeling the hard, crisp morning wind as it swept towards us, a lot colder than I remembered from the Africa of my youth. To my left, as the cold wind blew across the warm seventy-five-degree water, the spray plumed out from the waves as they reared up and broke, mixing with the mist rising off the water.

Caused by the temperature differential between the sea and the land, the ocean looked like it was steaming. Further out, across the broad expanse of the ocean, all the way to the horizon, the primeval African sun looked like it was boiling up out of the water, the blood-red orb connecting me to my homeland and to the days of my youth, when all that mattered was that next wave coming to me from over the horizon.

My friend and I paddled out together through the warm, clear water and started sharing waves as the dawn rolled away and the African sun rose higher. It was an interesting and challenging wave. The swell would bend in from the south and rise up steeply on the shallow reef. The takeover was vertical and very demanding for me, as most of the waves in California are generated from storms a long way away, so they come into the beach rather slowly.

Once I dropped in, these waves curved in at me, quick and fast, and threw out in a perfectly oval tube. On the long, hollow barrels you could drive hard, really pressure up the concave under the board to increase speed, and fly through the tube, then get blasted out with that faint spray of compressed air—what I call "the breath of God."

It had been some time since I had ridden great tubes, and a long time since I felt connected to the wave, to my past and to the present, and to the future that was just out of reach, represented by that slowly spinning oval that was just ahead of my board.

After a great ride, I paddled back to the takeoff, to where my pal was sitting. A couple of guys had joined us, and a southwesterly wind had started gently ruffling the groomed surface of the water. It was almost time for me to go, but before my last ride, I asked my friend the name of the break.

"We call it One Eye. When the wave breaks and the tube throws, it looks like an eye."

Surfers often conjure up descriptive names for the fearsome surf breaks they ride: Banzai Pipeline in Hawaii, Cyclops in Australia, and Mavericks in California.

One Eye. An apt name, I thought as I paddled for my last wave.

A long ride took me a hundred yards down the point, down to a place where the water was deeper, darker, and felt more dangerous.

I kicked out and began the lonely paddle back, and that familiar prickly sensation crawled up my spine and down my arms. Every surfer feels it at one time or another, that inescapable feeling that there is something large moving beneath the surface. I tried not to look down, but I had to, and I could see I had company just beneath my board, two long dark shapes moving with me, one on either side, as long as my board. I felt a moment of palpable, chilling fear, a gut-quivering dread of being consumed as prey, a feeling of absolute vulnerability and helplessness.

Suddenly, the water erupted on both sides of me and I froze, thinking it was all over.

Two dolphins leaped out of the water and into the air, showering me with spray. The relief was overwhelming, my fear of being ripped apart disappearing into the wind as joy overcame me—how good it was to be alive!

I took my last ride in and picked a path through the rocks along the shore. I walked up the beach, dripping wet, elated and satisfied, with a vestige of fear still remaining.

I walked past a man on the beach fishing with a large bamboo rod and a reel as big as a small car wheel—fishing for something large.

"You haven't been surfing out there, have you?" he asked.

"Well, what do you think?" I responded, smiling.

"Do you know what we call this place?" he asked.

"Yeah, you call it One Eye," I said.

"Do you know why we call it One Eye?" he asked.

"You call it One Eye because when the wave breaks, it looks like an eye," I answered.

"No. We call it One Eye because there is a big Zambezi shark that lives out there in the lineup, and when it rolls over on its side to bite, all you see is one eye . . ."

I laughed and walked back to the car thinking how two people can see reality so differently, how perspectives can differ so greatly.

This is a book of perspective—in the same way that the fisherman and I had different perspectives of the surf break, of the tube and shark, so too will you, the reader, have a different perspective than mine. This book is my perspective and Noah's, and our perspectives alone. Our words are meant to hopefully be a starting point to look a little differently at what you know. Do you focus on the positive or the negative? Do you live in joy or fear? Do you paddle in after a wipeout or paddle back out? Do you take every wave that comes your way or share some?

We want you to know, which we believe you understand, is that this book is **not** a prescription. We all make our own choices and decisions on which wave to catch and how we ride along the way. While this book contains some of the simple principles we have lived by, it also contains a perspective on the same core values and societal foundations that are as relevant today as when they were written thousands of years ago. We have tried to make sense of happiness and tragedy, success and failure, love and loss, which we have all experienced throughout life.

We have tried to describe what has kept us going when we have been absolutely devastated by the harsh winds of sorrow that have blown us off our feet. We are both deeply connected to the ocean, which has shaped our perspective and has been there for us every step of the way, helping mold us to see life a little differently and keep us motivated to look forward to the next wave.

I will finish with thoughts of a brisk morning, perhaps tomorrow, with the sun just rising at the edge of the horizon, where the Santa Ynez Mountains fold down towards the Pacific, under the rainbow bridge that connects all of us in our hometown of Santa Barbara and beyond, to the past, present, and future.

We hope that you have enjoyed the guide and the ride . . .

Shaun, the Surfer

SHAUN TOMSON, MARK RICHARDS AND
MARK WARREN AT OFF THE WALL, HAWAII

WAIMEA BAY, OAHU, HAWAII

THE SAGE

While we all like to have a summation, a bottom line, a clear conclusion that we can count on or look to, having a chapter entitled "A Final Perspective" is a contradiction in terms. Why? Well, because there is no finality. Finality is only a rumor born of perspective. When the sun goes down, it appears to go over the edge of things, but ask Columbus. The world is round and over the edge is only around the curve. Any line extended far enough into space will curve back on itself. There is no finality. Only continuance. No wave is final. Every wave that has ever been is again a wave in some form, in some sea of events. And you too!

When Shaun and I decided to do this book, that he was the Surfer was too obvious. Then Shaun said, "Noah, you are the Sage."

So, cast in this role by a friend's observation, what's the Sage's final word? It's this: Excuse what I have written here when I have been a fool. I am no longer young enough to know everything. What I know can fill a book. What I don't know can fill a library.

Thanks for your company in our guide. I hope you have found my words to be a source of strength. God knows we all need to be strong and a source of strength to others.

Visualize me touching my heart and pointing at you, saying "peace and blessings."

Noah, the Sage

PHOTO BY CHRIS ORWIG

ABOUT THE AUTHORS

Noah benShea is one of North America's most respected and beloved poet-philosophers. He is the Pulitzer Prize–nominated and internationally best-selling author of 29 books, translated into 18 languages and embraced around the world.

Shaun Tomson is a former World Surfing Champion and has been described as one of the greatest and most influential surfers of all time; he is an inductee in the US, Jewish, and South African Sports Halls of Fame. Shaun is also a world-renowned leadership mentor, entrepreneur, environmentalist, and best-selling author.

ABOUT FAMILIUS

VISIT OUR WEBSITE: WWW.FAMILIUS.COM

Familius is a global trade publishing company that publishes books and other content to help families be happy. We believe that the family is the fundamental unit of society and that happy families are the foundation of a happy life. We recognize that every family looks different, and we passionately believe in helping all families find greater joy. To that end, we publish books for children and adults that invite families to live the Familius Ten Habits of Happy Family Life: *love together, play together, learn together, work together, talk together, heal together, read together, eat together, give together* and *laugh together*. Founded in 2012, Familius is located in Sanger, California.

CONNECT

Facebook: www.facebook.com/familiustalk
Twitter: @familiustalk, @paterfamilius1
Pinterest: www.pinterest.com/familius
Instagram: @familiustalk

The most important work you ever do will be within the walls of your own home.

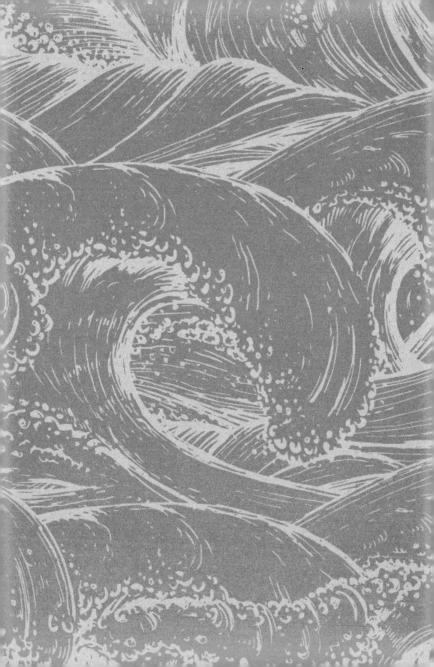